red, white, and blues

POEMS

SEAN MURPHY

Cover design by
Morgan Ryan
morganryancreative.com

Cover image by
Justen Ahren
justenahren.com

BRIGHT
MOMENTS
BOOKS

For Morgan, Mark, Ellie,

Jess, and Ashton:

a team of special people

doing extraordinary things

Author's Note

I wrote ***red, white, and blues*** because I believe poetry can still tell the truth when other forms have failed us. These poems are not interested in neutrality; they are interested in clarity. They move through history and pop culture because that is where our myths live—where power learns to hide and where harm learns to look inevitable. (I also have come to believe poetry is the best way to mash up history, media, political commentary, and a succinct formula for connecting dots in ways Op-Eds, fiction, and social media grandstanding can't and won't.)

These poems are political, name names, and while I don't have any illusions my modest efforts can affect the type of meaningful change we desperately need in America right now, this book is a flag flown in solidarity, and a middle finger to the establishment. As such, I think this collection coming into the world at the right time—and perhaps can inspire some dialogue or instigate something positive.

I wanted to write a book that calls out what we worship, what we excuse, and what we leave behind, while still honoring the strange, stubborn beauty that survives in language. If these poems confront, I hope they also invite conversation. If they provoke, I hope they also connect. Art matters because it reminds us that we are not alone in our witnessing.

February, 2026

Contents

It is difficult to get the news from poems,
yet men die miserably every day for lack of
what is found there.

—William Carlos Williams

Adam's Apple Blues

for Anthony Bourdain

Meats of many flavors, lush grapes stomped
with stained heels, vegetables bursting out
of the ground like inverted lightning bolts,
the toilsome ingenuity of rolled tobacco, or
the way beans can become something else,
providing hope for the most hellish hangovers:
all these are fodder for unquenchable appetites,
an addiction wherein excess does not diminish;
unless you consider it likely drove Adam insane—
tasting everything for the first time as it exploded
into life all around him—being ordered to abjure
temptations that made him father to starving sons,
and forsaking the fruits from a god who exiled him,
breaking this world He made—in order to save it.

Christopher Columbus's Mermaids*

Not half as beautiful as they are painted...

He described the same false sirens so many
others had sworn seeing: creatures familiar
not by sight so much as invocation; stories
recycled through centuries about the beautiful
half-humans who lived amongst their cold-blooded
cousins, tails that turned to flesh if taken ashore.

Such absurdity, both fabrication and fancy, says much
about libidinous men who stared too long at nothing
but brutal blue horizons, unbroken in every direction.

What of the breasts, they lamented, seeing little
but scales and whiskers, more man than fish; nothing
at all like a woman—much less a dream to get lost in.

And during the last stretch of more lonely days at sea,
they became yet another miracle that wouldn't materialize,
not unlike those new lands decreed by divine providence.

(*In 1493, during his voyage that led him to the "New World," Christopher Columbus described three "mermaids"—which were in all likelihood manatees—as "not half as beautiful as they are painted.")

Captain Cook's Chimera*

Did some of the more romantic
amongst them occasionally wonder
if there was life beyond their island?
With no war to fight, did those inclined
to violence become complacent?
Were those stars that shot beyond
an unblemished sky signs of some kind
of some celestial intelligence; of gods
watching and knowing they were being
watched? Could there be unknown spells
on offer from strangers who did not die?

(* On January 18, 1778, the English explorer James Cook becomes the first European to travel to the Hawaiian islands; his crew were initially welcomed, and it is suspected the Hawaiians attached religious significance to the first stay of Europeans on their islands. After one of the crewmembers died, exposing the Europeans as mere mortals, relations became strained.)

George Custer's Courage*

If the best we can say about someone
when he's no longer around to speak
for himself is: *he didn't lack courage*,
this is not only the most vacant praise,
it obviates all the consequential things
for which the use of courage is required.

(*After the government convicted Custer of desertion and mistreatment of soldiers earlier that year in a military court, and despite his unpopularity, he was considered a good fighter. On November 27, 1868, Custer leads an early morning attack on a band of peaceful Cheyenne, hailed as the first substantial American victory in the Indian wars—and restoring the colonel's reputation.)

King Leopold's Conquest

after *Heart of Darkness*

Greatness does not wait
for permission or approval.

Fortune is not accrued
by consensus or equivocation.

Power does not apologize
for blood it expends like breath.

Empire must not interrogate
the means of its endowment.

Royalty spurns remonstration,
in thrall only to sacred edicts.

Causes need not requite
those they employ or destroy.

Dark hearts only demand
that the gold never gets cold.

Jack Johnson's Apostasy*

Even the most fervent might
begrudgingly accept
a black man
being heavyweight champion
because the Lord moves
in the most mysterious ways

(but that money, that car, those women)

and even God was entitled
to watch what he created
and for better or worse
allow all sorts of sin and impiety

(think of Saul or Magdalene or Christ Himself)

or perhaps it occurred, at last—
as he saw us not seeing
Him or following the prescribed path—
if this is the way
you people handle your affairs,
if this is what's become
of the world I created,
with my eternal hands
I wash them of you.

(*Jack Johnson, nicknamed the "Galveston Giant," became the first black world heavyweight boxing champion in 1908. His success against white fighters and relationships with white women earned him scorn and instigated racial riots, including police harassment under the Federal Mann Act, causing him to flee the country to avoid imprisonment.)

Jake Gittes's Nose

after *Chinatown*

The bad guys always get away with it, obviously—
as criminal enterprises are often incestuous affairs.

And the rare exceptions to the rule only ensure
those clever or corrupt or ruthless enough are
capable of…*anything*, including owning police.

If you can't bring the desert to the city, bring the city
to the sea: complete God's work—or at least Cortez's.

Everyone knows a fish rots from the head—
but think of the future, and never forget you can't
smell anything if you've lost your nose.

A horse will lead you to water, but we die of thirst
searching, not aware that we've already drowned.

Willy Loman's Life

after *Death of a Salesman*

Nobody's worth nothing
dead, some insist. And deep
jungles are full of diamonds—
but only if you can steal them.

There's a secret they never tell you,
which is this: you have to sell yourself
to yourself, but to believe it you deny
the dream you've already been sold.

The life of a salesman?
Nothing is free anywhere—
everything alive survives in the wild
with a trade-off. After all:
what are predators but peddlers of a sort,
working their territories, waiting and preying,
closing in for the kill so they'll eat,
then do it all over again, until one day,
at last, they can't?

Harry Anslinger's Song*

Reefer makes darkies think they're as good as white men.

—Harry J. Anslinger

You can look it up: this feverish G-Man was a hunter
of illicit drug fiends, concentrated mostly on cannabis
—as they called it back in the not-so-great old days,
and he saw it as his mission to separate the wicked
weed from upstanding (see: white) citizens, *et cetera.*

If it's obvious now, one wonders what it was, then
that he—like every zealot who becomes obsessed
with sins (invented or else described in the bible)—
wasn't merely suppressing, but broadcasting his own
fears, as sanctimonious men tend to do with impunity.

Intoxicated by the rot of his time, it was black heads
he had in his sights, particularly the jazz musicians
whose brilliance belied those aberrations of racism:
thus Billie Holiday, handcuffed and helpless as she lay
dying, a preemptive strike for the FBI's work-in-progress.

So: who would it surprise this crusader was complacent
about morphine when he found himself facing the music;
amenable, too, to helping his partner in crime, who saw red
everywhere—on account of his bloodshot eyes—mitigate
the verdict in his head that wasn't even waiting for history?

(*Anslinger served as the first commissioner of the Federal Bureau of Narcotics, supporting prohibition and the criminalization of drugs, using his position to target and harass jazz musicians. As his health declined, he used morphine to manage his own pain, and provided his friend, the disgraced—and addicted—Senator Joseph McCarthy, with his own supply.)

Charles Mingus's Cry*

There's the day the most enthusiastic, even smug jazz obsessive realizes—although he's been listening for years and processed the miracle of five men making all this racket—as that epic bass solo winds down and the band returns to the battlefield, that surreal shrieking that bursts forth, splattering the horns like lamb's blood is, in fact, Mingus himself, hollering as he did; and perhaps it's at this moment one wonders *holy hell how did he imitate a muted trumpet so uncannily, so perfectly* only to understand, at last: this is not a man mimicking the urgent wail of brass and air, it's the instruments that are translating sounds wounded men have been making for centuries.

(*Of "Haitian Fight Song," the opening track from Charles Mingus's 1957 album *The Clown*, the composer wrote "I can't play it right unless I'm thinking about prejudice and hate and persecution, and how unfair it is. There's sadness and cries in it, but also determination.")

Charles Mingus's Metaphor

He really knew now. He really knew.

—Charles Mingus, *The Clown*

Charles Mingus made five albums in 1957, and the first one he recorded was *The Clown*. He called it *The Clown* because the title track was also a mission statement. He called it *The Clown* because he knew artists sometimes frighten the people who pay them. He called it *The Clown* because he cherished the dividends an apt metaphor can provide. He called it *The Clown* because the only thing heavier than his smile was his sorrow. He called it *The Clown* because he understood performing tricks often makes the wrong people laugh. He called it *The Clown* because look at the album cover. He called it *The Clown* because he knew most of us want to see how the magic works—until we've seen it.

Thelonious Monk's Movement*

What, you don't believe
God danced?

Looking down and around,
at all this color & sound,

including all those things
even He couldn't see,

maybe a little bit scared
he'd outsmarted Himself—

this first improvisation,
an entire world unfurled

from inside a mind
that didn't know how to sleep;

it could only keep on
creating, thinking, loving,

the messenger the same
as the message,

aware, at last,
that it was up to no one

or nothing else
to keep everything alive.

(*Thelonious Monk, the brilliant, eccentric jazz composer was known for getting up from his piano during live performances and dancing around the stage while his bandmates continued playing.)

Curtis Mayfield's Construction

Civil rights on the radar, and art becoming something more than what it had been, an era when suddenly songs were crafted the way we once built cathedrals: with carefully cultivated precision, and unflinching belief in the purpose of an endeavor—like being called to war or converting unawakened souls. Every stone in its place, stained glass inserted with the type of meticulous patience nature requires to repopulate burned out forests. Enormous slabs of marble cut into impossible angles, and always the presumed presence of saints blessing the proceedings. Enter St. Curtis—not yet Super Fly but actively metamorphosizing into something extra, something beyond what even he might have imagined—obliged to make men's flesh do indescribable things with the instruments of their invention, a foundation meant to expand after its completion; music's magic being the fact that it's never finished.

Muhammad Ali's Induction*

It must have been something to stand,
looking out at the smoke-lit masses,
most dressed for weddings (or, more appropriately,
a funeral), having thrown down dough
and placed their best bets on which black man
would beat the other's brains in, alive at the end
of fifteen rounds (if necessary), to be crowned
king of the ring, and realize: these men could
make or lose money on what you did with your fists
& those same hands aren't fit to shake or touch their wives,
or do anything other than serve for or clean up after them,
the same as it always was until certain gullible types,
guilt-ridden about God's will, turned this country inside
out—and where does it end, lying down with animals?

It must have been something to know
these same folks—most safely past draft age—
would see the flag to which they pledged allegiance
happy fighting to the last drop of others' blood
& stay heavyweight champion of the world,
also KOing the proliferation of Communist rebellion,
a kind of one-two punch to sustain a great white hype,
reminding the uppity ones about their place
and why they best be content w/ table scraps,
all other things considered, and had a few battles
in the South gone differently we wouldn't be in this mess,
and how dare you even think twice about who's in charge
and writes the checks; don't forget:
you get made and you can get unmade—
that's the American Way.

(*On April 28, 1967, with the United States at war in Vietnam, boxing champion Muhammad Ali refused to be inducted into the armed forces, saying "I ain't got no quarrel with those Vietcong." Ali was convicted of draft evasion, stripped of his title, sentenced to five years in prison, and banned from boxing for three years.)

Richard Nixon's Fix

I desire to serve God and to grow rich,

like all men.

—John Converse

after *Who'll Stop the Rain*

Fuck real life
is what Tuesday Weld says,
junked up & blissed out,
to an impossibly young Nick Nolte,
who'd never again be so thin
(or young, or able to die, on screen, too soon):
a steady diet of tai chi and Wild Turkey,
the kind of soldier who could dance
in the face of death, mercenary style:
murder served up like pizza delivery
or a drug deal gone awry, and how else
could it go down, amateurs hoping to make a killing
in the rigged field of fire—entirely too much
money at stake, like any scam or war?

Who'll stop the rain
the movie asks, rhetorically,
PFC Fogerty having already done his part:
heavy lifting, lyrically, wars always there
as fodder for metaphors about life & death
and other games men play,
except the stakes felt staler in '69,

stateside, where well oiled & indifferent
citizens held silver sun reflectors
to get more light—since it's never cloudy
in California (or anywhere you can avoid
the draft), a new Empire-in-Progress
starring cigarette smoke as incense
and shirtless men standing on lawns
dry as their martinis, grass & pools dying
for a larger cause so Americans could
live long if not prosper, another metaphor
that might kill you, like narcotics or napalm.

This is where everyone finds out who they are
is what MIAs say, at least to themselves.
Truth is, it's all war all the time:
overseas or at home, the *dog days*
they used to say, but now it never stops
raining and even the dogs today are harder,
stale chow still free & softer than survival
in the wild, killing whatever you ate—
until man & beast evolved into whatever it is
we've become, making careers out of combat
and the only drug on offer the same prize
it's always been: staying alive,
which—all the screenplays remind us—
remains the most enticing high
existence serves up, for free & forever.

Henry Kissinger's CV

Ambassador:

Tainted midwife to travesty, a perverted Prometheus, bestowing agency to perfidious officials in conspicuous places.

Instigator:

Slick devil whispering nothing's sweet, so many iniquitous seductions into the eager ears of meager men.

Bootlicker:

Fattened tongue sucking the leathered paws of a cur whose wet scent still befouls a nation's hollow halls.

Confessor:

Aberrant principles unshackled by access to brokers of action breaking worlds like sadistic gods with glimmering eyes.

Profiteer:

Thirty pieces of soiled silver times thirty a thousand times, it profits a man immeasurably if he has no soul to lose.

Sloganeer:

Peace through power, clarity through chaos, obedience through atrocity, efficiency through occupation, *et cetera.*

Impregnator:

Malevolent proposals polluted by your corrupted seed, so much ruthless sperm seeking attainment in lethal deeds.

Clock-Ticker:

Grown engorged like an unkillable tick, the mother's milk of abandoned empires a mainline to an obstinate heart.

Idolator:

Squatting on the shoulders of moral dwarves, the not-so-complex imprimatur of Napoleon your obscene escutcheon.

Kissinger:

This crass pageant, at long last, expired: ignominy awaits and History's already at work, unkindly revising the Final Cut.

Colonel Kilgore's Concerto

after *Apocalypse Now*

When the fat lady finally sings it reminds us that Wagner's operas—which, aside from conquest, were in some quarters considered the singular height of human achievement—tended to celebrate not only war, but war amongst the gods, and more, the twilight of those gods, signaling it was time, at last, for heroes on earth.

When the fat lady sings it reminds us that even in the 20th Century Wagner's operas, in some quarters, signified that empire was waning, or final solutions needed implementing—depending on which biographies have been updated, which news outlets one relies on, or which political party is inspiring a new kind of recruit for the cause.

When the fat lady sings it's the militant score for a movie, and once—depending upon what books one reads—served as a soundtrack inspiring if not celebrating murder (of Jews, amongst gods); but mostly, for the purposes of this poem, the fat lady's song provides the soundtrack to accompany a massacre, itself a reminder that Charlie don't surf.

Sergeant Elias's Sacrifice

after *Platoon*

Naturally, Sgt. Elias is destined to die.

We know this from the very first frame:
Him the muddy angel, all impossible
white teeth, smiling down at poor Taylor
(whom we know is going to live, this being
a movie, after all); the boy who will bear
arms, bear witness, and live to become
a director for whom Willem Dafoe is
more or less a delivery device—*the scene:*
scripted to solicit an Academy Award
the way tricks sniff dimly-lit streets,
foxholes filled with friendly fire
and love only money can buy.

Even if you're slow on the uptake
(say 16 years old and either corruptible
or capable of seeing the light shined
by a born-again grunt), of course
by the time Elias defies Barnes—
and defines the lost cause he alone
is capable of seeing as the charade it was—
we know it's all over but the shooting…

But which shot kills him?

It isn't the one from his brother in arms (not
named Cain because even for Oliver Stone
that would have been a bit much), or the first
flurry from the foes who, we will eventually
appreciate, weren't or shouldn't or might not
have been enemies at all, except for the plans
of reckless & highly decorated men with polished
shoes sitting behind desks scattered with binders,

detailing strategy and stating acceptable casualties.

It's meant to be shocking when Elias dies, his iconic
transfiguration storyboarded like an Olympic routine,
making ballet out of butchery the way war movies do.

He'd get his chance to play Christ for Scorsese
(coming down from the cross to briefly be a man); here
he *is* Christ, arms akimbo—and stretched to the sky,
dying for our sins, obviously, his fate foreshadowed
that time he watched the stars, one falling as if to say:
this is you, but also what you'll *be*: bright, brief, eternal.

And speaking of sins, wasn't Elias KIA before he ever
set foot in The Shit? Before he and The System locked horns
to see who would gain control of Charlie Sheen's soul?
Before he enlisted or was drafted and even before he was
born? Because there have always been superior officers
sending young men into strange places to fight or die—
trying to win something they can never quite define.

Freedom? Peace? Or another chapter in another book
to remain unread by all the people for whom it was written?

And who are we to blame the men whose burden it is
to order death if they believe what it is they're doing?

And you? Do you believe?

In '86? Yeah.

Now? No.

Pol Pot's Purgatory

On April 15, 1998, under house arrest, Pol Pot dies in his sleep, apparently of natural causes.

One reads that and thinks: there truly is no God,
no justice, no sense, no anything fair or good.

A remorseless murderer, passing in his sleep
and not hanging upside down, his internal organs
splashed in a red pool beneath him, the engine
of what made his sadistic system run the last thing
he'd ever see? Not alone, shivering, in a darkened,
dank jail cell, or else on the public square, the sounds
of jeering survivors hastening his descent to Hell?

But let's consider what often occurs when we're not
awake: dreams, which don't always accommodate
our private hopes and hungers; even the quietest brain
can't quell the messy machinery of the mind's biology,
and perhaps the most sanguine psychopath still broods,
knowing that power without peace and silence without
consent is an ersatz state of affairs, that being feared,
through intimidation, brings neither peace nor purpose.

And perhaps it's only at night, alone and unprotected,
while in the grip of forces that control craven tyrants
and their puny designs, the balance is laid bare—
this is where an evil soul is imprisoned, powerless
to prevent or escape the cascading spiritual horrors
that exist only in the killing fields of the mind, forever.

Pam Grier's Perm

It wasn't a halo so much
as her statement of purpose.

A permanent statement
or purposeful state of mind.

Which is what the '70s were:
a decade where black was not

only beautiful, but exploited
as such, and if soul could sell

we got on that train and danced
all the way to the bottom line,

which is a woman's best assets,
or whatever keeps the lights on.

A sister could own her own sex
and then copyright that shit

so prurient folks will pay—
any short cut to Brown Sugar

which, in America, never is out
of style, since it's the tasteless

that decide who's in the club—
b/c it's still a man's world after all,

worse still, a white man's world—
and what's worse than white men

trying to tell the rest of us what's hip?
But brothers of all colors understand

which kinds of bodies never come

with an expiration date: true miracles

live forever, preserved in motion
pictures realer than reality & more foxy

than anything; our ridiculous dreams
no match for what God or Satan created:

a fantasy made of flesh & blood, this vision
you somehow see best with your eyes shut.

Evel Knievel's Nuts

That's what everyone said: the guy's nuts. But there's good money in being crazy, the only catch being you have to survive in order to spend it. Bones, like records, are meant to broken, assuming you're the one doing the breaking (also, using a baseball bat on another man is simply bad business). You have to not care just enough, and that's the difference between clearing a jump and ending up with your ass broken in Snake River Canyon. Or with portions of yourself you can't afford to lose spread along the asphalt at Caesar's Palace. To do that kind of damage one must already be impaired in ways paying crowds can't see on TV. But that's part of what being a man is, or at least certain types of men. The type of man, for instance, who jumps the Grand Canyon. Or the men who enlist for war then go back for more, not for money or even so-called glory, but because there's a juice to that action civilian life can't approximate. Or bank robbers: they need the bread, but there are other ways to rip off the system; part of the fun, they know, is the thrill of the chase, the uncertainty of making it out alive. Also knowing, in advance, that no one gets out of this mess still breathing, no matter how hard we pray death away. And most of all, avoiding any career run by clocks, which leave you for dead long before you're underground. Only a handful ever figure out you're not truly alive until people know you by a nickname. And if you occasionally prove what goes up doesn't necessarily come down, you'll live forever.

Chuck Barris's Blow

You blew it.

All that money,
the power,
your potential.

Down the drained
bank account.

Ratings & pay raises
will fly, then die:

like the most expensive snow,
or tolerance for the tedium
of idiots being exploited.

You could smell the candy:
how and by whom we desire
to be distracted;
all in a life's work.

The nose knows.

If it can't smell shit,
it's up to the individual
to say if they trust their taste.

You were rarely wrong
as it related to the hoi polloi,
and what it might hoover up
during prime time.

The nose isn't unlike a mouth:
it too has an appetite—
and this hunger is not a metaphor,
it describes everything
you can't cook in an oven,
all that fits inside
a dangerous mind.

You sucked
the marrow out of life,
as Thoreau admonished.

And your highs & lows
confirmed there's plenty

to mainline in this life—

depending upon where you fall
within the food chain.

Boundaries bludgeoned,
career as running commentary
on culture, deadened senses, etc.

Or was it all a confession?

Obliging critics
and even the long-
gonged to inquire
which came first:

The Chicken or The End

of western civilization?

(*Chuck Barris was an American game show creator, producer, author, and host of *The Gong Show*, a provocatively lowbrow showcase for public humiliation, now recognized as a precursor to 21st Century reality TV trends.)

Ronald Reagan's Revolution*

Dead, at last; drowned in a bathtub,
this beast shrinks within itself until
there's nothing left but the esurience
of what killed it—an ethos: fear itself.

(*Grover Norquist, an American political analyst and anti-tax advocate, founded Americans for Tax Reform in 1985 and later declared "I don't want to abolish government; I simply want to reduce it to the size where I can drag it into the bathroom and drown it in the bathtub.")

Gordon Gekko's Greed

after *Wall Street*

This is some off-menu, Members Only shit:
the 1980's as apotheosis; a white (collar) plate
special popping Alan Greenspan's portfolio
& Pat Riley's panache inside a food processor.

Allergic to accountability and seasoned liberally
(get it?) with Voodoo Economics and readymade,
if blandly artificial flavoring, bear market broth
& a dollop of deregulation served with good whine.

Add in entitlement with a side-dish of the death tax,
and good old boy networking (not racist, naturally,
I always pick the best man for the job, he'd say—
and it's not my fault if all the candidates belong

To my country club, besides, you think it's easy
having to deal with all these Jew bankers?),
skipped breakfasts and liquid lunches toasting liquidity,
harried affairs, foxes, buds & balls broken like so many

Promises made with crossed fingers and averted eyes,
dotted-lines signed and mortgages refied; all in a stock
shortened with enough blow to break the sinuses of a city
that never sleeps, and where everyone knows: Greed is God.

Roy Cohn's Clients*

A fact: misery loves company, and to get the goods one follows the money, figures out whatever it is motivating those with means who can either afford to forget or forgo lessons learned. Who else could represent the media, the clergy, and the mafia but a lawyer? And not just any lawyer, but one who understood money gives you skin like a walrus, able to withstand the jaws of the law, ethics committees, and the outrage of law-abiding imbeciles. It's a club, strictly business (except it's also so personal you can never tell anyone what's happening behind the scenes), and to be admitted means never having to ask; means you were born into it, a kind of anti-royalty where you swim within the blood of the starving class. The only catch which, of course, has been applicable for free and forever, is that as light slips into night you'll still die alone, knowing there's no one to call on as misery—which enjoyed the company of your short life—is the only thing you can rely on, and in those last moments it demands an accounting for the black magic it eternally inspires in empty men who break the world to feed a nothing that feasts on itself.

(*Roy Cohn's clients included Condé Nast magazines; the Catholic Archdiocese of New York; the Ford Model Agency; Studio 54; Potamkin Cadillac; Baron di Portanova; Donald Trump; Warren Avis; and a long list of mob bosses such as "Fat Tony" Salerno and Carlo Gambino.)

Rodney King's Cameo*

These days we say *video or it didn't happen*
but back then even if recorded it didn't mean
it happened, because what's a crime's is often
in the eye of the beholder, but also in the eyes
of whoever helps package & present The News
in the bowels of a major news network, serving up
a reality open to interpretation, also with an eye toward
key demographics and subscribers and advertisers
and blowback from folks who routinely write letters
to the editor, using a familiar script asking, indignantly,
why we can't just get back to *the way it was*, then—
when people feared God and understood everything
that goes down here is just a preview, an audition
for the main event, the chosen few so many meteorologists
explaining that just because it's raining today
the sun's set to come out, eventually, and if they can
convince enough people they are appealing enough
they could be promoted to the role of anchor, the voice
of God on this earth that millions listen to every night
occasionally scaring us about *the way it is*, but mostly
promising if we keep hope alive everything will be OK.

(*On March 3, 1991, Rodney King leads police on an 8-mile pursuit through Los Angeles, California, before being stopped and brutally beaten by several white police officers. The incident was captured on video and sold to local TV station KTLA, which broadcast the footage, triggering a national outcry—and initiating a debate about police brutality.)

Freddie Mercury's Magic

Goodbye, everybody: I've got to go / Gotta leave you all behind and face the truth.

—Queen

There was nothing Bohemian about the early 90s: a rhapsody of dollar drafts, pegged jeans, and happy hours featuring free wings, hairspray, Drakkar Noir, and other chemically assembled abominations. And smoke, always the smoke; we knew it was going to kill us, but so was everything else, like wars and politicians and day jobs and cops and, all of a sudden, simply having sex. Keep yourself alive? We thought we were all going to die, even or especially the compulsive sorts who actually wore condoms. Here we were, caught in a landslide called *fin de siècle* and suddenly this insanity from Africa (where, we'd learned in college, everything came from anyway, no matter what motion pictures or the bible said). A kind of magic: monkey business always a big hit in America. Crazy little thing: the planet finally wiped out, for love no less (or at least fucking, which is what we lived for in the first place). Why us, we cried, thinking of the 60s—or even the 80s—when sex was expensive but seldom an accessory, a little body language now a matter of life and death. What had we wrought? Rock not so hard after all, and if movie stars could die, what hope did frat boys have? Magic was tragic: even sports gods getting waylaid by weird science. Play the Game, a motto for every anonymous romp, experiments some of us hoped might lead to something more serious, not marriage so much as monogamy, where we could be the heroes of our own stories, the lives we saved our own, et cetera. The show must go on, we knew—so we drank & rode dirty, hangovers now including the occasional blood test at a free clinic (stay positive, we didn't say). Is this the real life? Russian Roulette in the sheets and nuclear winter in our shorts. Joking about the *gay flu* not so funny anymore (Spare him his life from this monstrosity!); nothing really matters until a hijacked plane crashes in your back yard, all of us potential terrorists hoping a little STD might be as bad as it ever got. Just Say No, we couldn't say, and it seemed like all the dead ancestors were biting back, a reminder of medieval times when plagues ate your face and wiped-out world history. Who wants to live forever, we boasted, half in the bag, all judgment suspended so we could get in someone's pants. Don't stop me now, we pouted, willing to believe in God or even George Bush if that would buy us more time. Another one bites the dust: everything commercials & songs taught us to demand ending us before lethargy or adulthood even had a chance. I want it all, each of us declared in our own style, hoping Freddie had taken one for the team, a dirty saint made to suffer so we could sin on, lip synching his songs as we drove blind toward whatever destiny had designed.

B.B. King's Blues

I hope you'll agree I've earned the right, B.B. King would say, after taking a seat shortly into his set, and the crowd, mostly white, leaning young, let him know with their applause, that they approved. Had he earned this indulgence—if such a graceful request could be so described? Who were we to say, how were we to know. This modest giant seated on his humble throne talking of the privileges he'd paid for, every moment of his life and counting, and that he wasn't speaking only of himself but for kindred spirits not in attendance, many already departed for pastures more peaceful than the ones they found here on planet earth, especially stateside, more specifically the deepest states south of Mason/Dixon. King was testifying for fellow travelers, all of whom had endured the worst the 20th Century offered black men and women, not least those who dared perform in public during a time it wasn't safe to be in certain spots after dark. These unassuming deities suffered indignity, mostly in silence (unable to do much because even doing very little was risky for well-meaning white folks back when), saving the sounds and fury for hollers buried in the grooves of vinyl, spinning sense into a backward world through the force of physics and magic. And time, which is the only thing the oppressed have ever had to give or bargain with. And these same folks, some of whom now appear on postage stamps, left artistic deposits still earning interest, not excluding the same hard cases who stood in their way, barring doorways and burning exits. It's all there in the music, but not everyone is born to sing and some of the best songs die, unheard in darkness, which is why the blues is a symptom and a cause and a cure and also something that can never be explained; the blues describe the unspeakable and somehow make you dance and sing and cry. The blues means you can forgive but you will not forget, and a declaration that becoming a saint does not make you less human and dying only means the suffering stops for all the wrong reasons. The blues tells a never-ending story about what the race line means and why we'll never be a colorblind society. The blues offers anyone who neither has nor understands the blues an abiding invitation to kindly shut the fuck up. The blues means turning blood into something sweeter than wine and earns you admittance into a club more exclusive than heaven, a sacred place where the band plays forever and never apologizes for getting old or sitting down. And mostly the blues means white people should never stop listening whenever a black person talks about the blues.

Rudy Giuliani's Reward*

after Chester Higgins's *Bowery Denizen, 1985*

Those fingers: holding neither money nor a wallet hoarding it
(*hold*, as in the verb meaning to carry, to possess; also to hold,
as in keep safe, the way banks hold deposits like promises kept,
the way he can't hold his liquor or too many times he was caught
holding drugs, or holding up his hands as if to say "hold it,"
showing he wasn't holding a gun, was not holding anything
that could hurt anything worse than he'd hurt himself, on the street
at all hours because he can't hold a job, the system with a hold on him,
meaning he's logged some hours in the holding tank, being held
on suspicion of murder or vagrancy, laws holding him accountable).

Hold on: is this because he wasn't held by his mother; why he can't
hold his ex-wife but knows to hold his tongue, the same way he holds
his spot in line, waiting for a hot meal or cold cup of coffee, holding
his coat during a warm day in autumn knowing he'll need it that night,
holding it close so nobody else steals it while he's holding something
else, like hope, with his hand held out for spare change—the dirty skin
creased, chapped, and cracked during evenings when heavy skies hold
snow— held in contempt by those who presume what his future holds,
or assure him that Christ is holding a place in heaven for every sinner:
our reward for living in a world unable to hold the weight of its pain?

(*Successfully campaigning on being "tough on crime," Rudy Giuliani became mayor of New York City in 1993. During his administration, city services for the impoverished were dramatically reduced, while arrests increased—leading to charges of racial profiling and suspicion that these efforts were intended less to help than to remove the homeless from public spaces, particularly in affluent areas.)

Allen Iverson's Answer

That crossover broke knees like a gangster
and could kill fools, snapping necks like nuts
when they followed his body and not the ball.

Number 3 broke other things too, like barriers
and bank vaults, dress codes, dogma & decorum,
and especially how old school saw The Game.

His ink like 'hood hieroglyphics, his lithe body
unbreakable—carrying the burden of weak teams
and an unwitting culture like a cross of gold.

Too sincere to signify, too perfect for *practice*;
where he came from every second's an audition
to see which ones were strong enough to survive.

He shot to score, rocked that bling to escape
incarceration, wore swagger like a security blanket
to keep sticky fingers out of his swollen pockets.

Every baller knows: the real thugs in this world
wear suits and strafe locker rooms w/ friendly fire,
their diet a steady buffet of black & broken hearts.

The way to stay rich is give 'til it heals, pay it
forward, drop deep bombs & trust your blood
is truer than the hyped ink, red in history books.

Howard Dean's Scream*

Was this the moment we shattered
the looking glass: seeing ourselves
but darkly; barely able to hear
talking heads above that scream—
not one voice, but the collective gasp
of an empire imploding, or surrendering;
needing so many things—to be entertained
above all, our boredom a breeding ground
for some virus that sustains then devours,
the spectacle of us feasting on ourselves
spun nightly via satellite from a TV studio?

Or four years before, when five justices stood
on the scale, appointed judges paid to pretend
being impartial, their unaccountable ruling
a preemptive strike against chimerical activism?

Or when a slick lawyer from Arkansas agonized
with consultants to drown our political discourse
in semantics, hastening our reluctant arrival
nowhere, debating what the meaning of *is* is?

Or when administration officials traded arms,
it suddenly being good business to do business
with bad guys—so long as The Gipper answered
every question in front of an American flag?

Or the regrettable evening a former peanut farmer
spoke to Americans like adults—this equanimity
unforgivable; shame and the lack of cynicism
a losing combination for fin de siècle malaise?

Was it the botched burglary at an elegant hotel?
Was it whatever really happened that day in Dallas?
Was it the Ohio Gang immortalizing blood for oil?
Was it that assassin's bullet in Lincoln's brain?

Or the bloodied axe of our founding father,
his cherry tree shading the unburied bodies
of the vanquished men who welcomed and taught
us to turn this hard soil into a seasonal harvest?

(*During a rally on January 19, 2004, Democrat Howard Dean—an outspoken critic of the Iraq War—was recorded encouraging supporters when his voice cracked; isolated audio was quickly sensationalized as the "Dean Scream," and became a central distraction for several days, providing welcome ammunition for Dean's opponents in both parties.)

The Decider's Decision

I'm the decider, and I decide what is best.

—George W. Bush

Tell us again

about the time

your higher father

told you your duty

was to believe

in the ax, again,

against an axis

of evildoers, who

sinned first, tempting

a nation trained not

to turn the other cheek,

and how your apostles

advocated for you and

the use of force that could

be called *biblical*, sending

enemies to the stone age—

when the one closest to you

kissed your ear with kind words

and turned salty water into

wine, this act of betrayal

the offense countless

inculpable families would

die to redeem, all so oil

might flow like tainted blood.

(*Journalist Bob Woodward asked Bush whether he consulted with his father before making the decision to go to war. "I don't remember. I could ask him and see if he remembers something," Bush said. "I'm not trying to be evasive. You know, he is the wrong father to appeal to in terms of strength. There is a higher father that I appeal to.")

Donald Rumsfeld's Romp*

Of course, we all saw the same images
and felt sickened, as any sensible person
would be by a display of such belligerence
and depravity; whatever always happens
when there's too much power and a void
of supervision, the way goldfish allegedly
will eat themselves to death if indulged
by a child who doesn't know any better.

But some of us saw something else, seeing
the photos of these young American soldiers
leading naked men around like docile dogs
(and the fear in their eyes, the money shot
every fascist impulse craves, to not only terrify
but humiliate—this is what can impel humans
to consider strangers from their same species
mere insects, something to be exterminated).

Some also saw the complacent certainty shared
by the architects of this fiasco, cocksure men
promising *they will welcome us as liberators,*
again stirring the scarcely-cooled cauldron
of indignity, sounding a familiar call to arms
and sending fresh soldiers overseas—to finish
what they didn't start so much as immortalize,
that eternal grievance measured in blood and oil.

(*On April 30, 2004, the CBS program *60 Minutes* reports on abuse of prisoners by American military forces at Abu Ghraib, a prison in Iraq. Photographs depicted American soldiers sexually assaulting detainees, threatening them with dogs, putting them on leashes and engaging in a number of other practices that clearly constituted torture and/or violations of the Geneva Convention.)

Mitch McConnell's Mini-Stroke

(A physician on Tuesday said Sen. Mitch McConnell, R-Ky., does not have a seizure disorder and did not have a stroke, with the confirmation coming after the Republican leader has frozen multiple times in front of reporters. From *USA Today*, September 5, 2023.)

He finds himself outside, not just outdoors but outside
Himself, in an alley that becomes something different,
something *more* during and especially after working hours,
in those hours when respectable sorts have eaten, bathed, prayed and retired
to the room where they sleep and do Anything
to avoid intimacy…

Another one steps forward, out of his shadow, buried beneath the building
(the building I've helped build, he thinks, not for the first time), voice urgent but lacking
any authority, laws and airtime the only means of accountability back here: *This
alley is where I* live, *motherfucker.*

And that hunger he's unable to sate, like a leash leading his
fleshy neck; that hunger, causing him to think insane thoughts
like: what if toes tasted like McNuggets made with actual chicken?

Shhhh, he replies, a soothing drawl, a voice marinated in money and the charcoaled
lungs of tobacco addicts, choking in tar and way too late for any lawsuit to save.

He leans in, advancing toward the sweaty and scabbed neck, his own throat
bobbing hungrily, almost amphibian; *this* is the type of transaction he requires
to stay alive, to remain engaged (engorged), to understand his nature and retain
belief in the inscrutable forces that have made men like him for centuries. He has….

So much work to do. It's endless, and none but him are able to answer this call…

Deep in the bowels of this building where the oiled chain of commerce churns…

He sits, unblinking, indefatigable, focused: another night without sleep or dreams.

Clarence Thomas's Conscience

I'm not my brother's keeper. It's right there
in the Good Book (you could have said ain't,
but you put away childish shit, I mean things,
or else they got whipped—from within.
That cautious cultivation of conscience:
You can't be right if you aren't righteous).

Nature proves nothing's natural; everything is
relative. There's always another Hill to climb.
And if some of those images can never be unseen,
that's strictly business between you and The Boss.
To endure dark thoughts is simple: submit
and let the stones be thrown—you're absolved.

The Man don't, I mean doesn't
give us nothing, I mean anything
we can't handle or don't deserve.
Technicolored folks or what some call
the whiter man's burden, idolators in denial,
are brought to justice, eventually, before our
Master, I mean Father, who sits beside
His son: the only Judge.

Betrayed by a kiss, learning nothing
anyone says can be assumed: even the ones
who honor you would see you strung up,
or sell you out, silver instead of salvation.
Just like those animals, I mean men, who prey
upon one another, enslaved in ghettos
of undisciplined thoughts and deeds.

Blaming a black man in a black gown, or
white men in white robes seems senseless,
like blaming clouds for rain, or fists for pain.
Virtue ain't got, I mean don't have, I mean
has not got a color, can you cotton to that?

Swine, shortenin' bread and a bag of shellfish, shit man,
I mean shucks, it's easy to slip up after you've sipped
a little too much blood turned to wining & dining.

Pride be damned, if you can rise above background
sometimes silence reveals more than speech.
A decision's pronounced regardless, so keep quiet,
I mean compliant, I mean principled.
A confession concealed
behind clenched teeth: Recalcitrance
that could almost be accused of being
spite—convicted again by those unblinking eyes.

Can you see the Boy you used to be,
reflected in the gleam of spit-shined shoes?
The same soles that have never walked
Forty Acres mule, I mean more—or less—
in their own footsteps?

Rupert Murdoch's Mutation

There are certain types of wasps
that systematically target spiders:

upon paralyzing them with a sting,
this predator neatly secretes her eggs.

These larvae, defying science or fiction, are
instinctually able to control the spider's brain;

the host oblivious until new life awakens,
slowly devouring it from the inside out.

After a while, unwitting progeny emerges
from a hollowed-out husk, an appropriation

which will recur—either until all's extinct,
or evolution accords a merciful remediation.

Joel Osteen's Soul

The wages of sin involve an inordinate faith—
how else to reconcile these words vs. deeds,
and so much industry in the service of oneself?

What, finally, is the more miraculous feat:
water to wine at a wedding, or favor gained
by fleecing one's spiritually-starved flock?

In a house thusly built (in the name of Our Father)
there are many mansions, havens prepared to repel
the unwashed—gates and guards to keep one safe.

In those halls are walls filled with money bloodily
wrung from disciples, whose spirits are scarred
from prayers unanswered and insults unredressed.

And these meek shall inherit the dearth, paradise lost
to finance extensions on churches filled past capacity,
presided over by profligate men with $500 haircuts.

Let us prey: God will help those who help themselves,
proselytizing a gospel of prosperity, sins redeemed for
untaxable alms recouping the apostasy of false prophets.

Donald Trump's Stakes

It's not that complex:
Quisling born rich without class,
Well-done, with ketchup.

St. James's Place*

Not only so, but we also glory in our sufferings, because we know that suffering produces perseverance.

—Romans 5:3

This city on the sea, reincarnated like a borrowed life: Babylon
redeemed by way of junk bonds, the world's eighth wonder—
according to He-Who-Didn't-Compensate-His-Contractors, busy
building anything but wealth, born off Broadway, blue-blooded
and blind to any colors on the wrong side of the strip: his palace,
courtesy of the Community Chest, all faux gold & laundered bills.

Here hotels were built and then abandoned, blithely named after
barons whose fortunes came and went—like trains moving money
and tourists from the boardwalk to more secure settlements
the salted waves won't reach: their utilities of inherited wealth
conceiving wholly new empires that extended from the ocean
to outer space, fresh time capsules incorruptible by commerce.

Casinos thrive as micro-monopolies: the rigged arenas of dreams
where gladiators die nightly, leaving emptied wallets in sad piles,
like so many bandages on a battlefield, these personal lotteries lost
one slow suicide at a time; the city finally a reflection of the system
it was built to sell, where fortunes are amassed faster than paychecks,
dynasties erected like pyramids, and the stock market is scientific fact.

This impossible promise ruined, patrolled now by cops & cab drivers;
pushers and pimps role-playing tokens, the forsaken streets creeping

with orphaned dogs amidst smoked out bars and boarded up buildings:
dinosaurs unaware the comet was coming, like some divine justice—
finally—as if Christ returned to the money taker's temple, flipping over
every blackjack table and consigning sweaty pit bosses to eternal fire.

Churches and funerals homes remain in business, starving with vacancies
for the converted or deceased as the least of our brothers, now ghosts,
cover the waterfront while mothers and sisters bear the burdens and babies,
keeping stillborn bloodlines from extinction, and silence herself gives last call
as the Eye in the Sky smiles down on James—patron saint of all who suffer—
reconciled to his place and begging forgiveness for those that trespass.

(*The properties in the board game Monopoly are named after streets in Atlantic City, N.J., famous in the early 20th Century for its beach and boardwalk. The tourist town eventually declined, and gambling was legalized in 1976, followed by high rises and casinos, several owned by real estate tycoon Donald Trump, who declared A.C. the eighth wonder of the world.)

Elon Musk's Assets

What's the point of having all those assets
if you're not willing to invest most of them
to develop a kind of liquidated virtual reality
that can be added to all the morphine drips
of born-again Christians—who've happily used
archaic biblical passages to bolster the unbelievable
interpretations of sex and race and salvation—
so that the last thing they see before they die
is Jesus, who of course is black, and then after
processing the shock and pain of this revelation,
another unwelcome vision proving God's a woman,
and finally, as they gasp through their last horrors,
a movie-version Moses who looks almost exactly
like Charlton Heston appears out of nowhere
to inform them, as he turns off the lights forever,
there never has been any heaven awaiting them?

Jeff Bezos's Billions

Billion-dollar babies are building their own toys,
taking them to outer space (inner space, of course,
that final frontier the wealthy will never breach).

The rest of us are stuck here on earth, amazed
and mystified by how humans understood shit
fertilized their fields, or how to create panacea
out of potatoes, or that, speaking again of waste,
we turned chamber pots into sewage systems—
the kind of revolution that launches rocket ships.

What we consume, recycled and repurposed,
still seems as miraculous as electricity or energy
derived from oil, a kind of anti-evolution wherein
we destroy this world by abusing what it produces.

Even to entrepreneurs or idealists, all this talk of exploring
other planets seems an obvious distraction to avoid
focusing on the one we actually inhabit, unwilling
to fix what we break while busy buying immortality.

Roy Batty's Tears

after *Blade Runner*

Tears in rain are like prodigal sons
in pain: lost without some purpose served;
useless in the end, even as parables.

Being more human than human: this is
an objective that's realized within dreams;
conceived only after empires have declined.

Memories are gifts, implanted by the men
making these machines, gods of Biomechanics
inaccessible in sky-scraping bedroom suites.

Time to die: a dilemma all creatures confront,
our mysteries unspooling by design, guided by
aloof grand masters higher up on the org chart.

Acknowledgments

"Willy Loman's Life": *The Adirondack Review*
"Rudy Giuliani's Reward," and "St. James's Place": *The Decadent Review*
"Muhammad Ali's Induction": *Words and Sports*
"Henry Kissinger's CV": *New Verse News*
"The Decider's Decision": *Wordpeace*
"Donald Trump's Stakes": *Exterminating Angel*
"Elon Musk's Assets": *Dumbo*

www.ingramcontent.com/pod-product-compliance
Lightning Source LLC
LaVergne TN
LVHW090136160826
845673LV00017B/2491

* 9 7 8 0 9 8 9 8 8 0 5 7 2 *